A

WORK

IN PROGRESS

JILLIAN SIGLER

ISBN 978-1-0980-3137-4 (paperback)
ISBN 978-1-0980-3138-1 (digital)

Christian Faith Publishing, Inc.
832 Park Avenue
Meadville, PA 16335
www.christianfaithpublishing.com

Printed in the United States of America

Contents

Introduction

*H*onesty beckons something deeper in someone. It builds connections with the people you allow into those hidden corners. I am a very honest person. I very rarely meet a stranger. If you know me, you know a piece of my story. I strive to be open and honest with everyone I meet. So with that being said, let me be honest with you.

I have no idea where this is going. I do not know what the next few pages hold in terms of their impact on you or your life. I feel as though the Father is teaching me daily how to glorify Him in the middle of it all. Whether stormy seas or cloudless skies, I want to sing praises to Him through it all.

However, it would be foolish of me to think that every day will be like this. That I will wake up every day for the rest of my life with this same spiritual awakening. Because I am human. I will falter. I will fail. I will not trust like I should. *But* that is the great beauty of our Savior. That even on the days when I do not love Him, He loves me. He is still there, calling me deeper into His love. And that is why I wanted to bring you along on my journey. To show you that it is okay to not always be excited to be on this journey. It is okay to feel lost, broken, and even alone. God's plan for your life is far more detailed than anything you could ever begin to articulate.

By no means am I writing this because I have my entire life figured out. I am not writing these poems because I have all the answers to life and how to be perfect. I am writing this book for the completely opposite reason: to show you that we are all imperfect. To show you that even on our best days, we can still fail. That we are always going to struggle *but* that we are loved by a loving God. A God that sees people in the worst shape of their lives and calls them to glorify Him. That on the days where my shirt is stained and my makeup isn't done, He calls me beautiful. He calls me worthy. He calls me His. I am a work in progress. This book is meant to show you just that. That it is okay to be called and still not know where we are called to. Just like me, this book of poems is a work in progress. These chapters have been accumulating over the years in the form of blog posts, poems, Instagram stories, Facebook posts, etc. I wanted this book to compile it all, and my hope is that you get something out of it. That you feel understood. That you feel valued.

Why Poetry?

I think poetry is one of the most beautiful mediums by which we can express our innermost thoughts and desires. I began to develop a love for poetry at a young age. I was fascinated by books, authors, poets, anyone who wrote words on a page and made them flow eloquently together. Through times of hardship, loss, defeat, growth, joy, and praise, I found myself writing.

Writing what the hurt felt like.

Writing how the joy danced in my heart.

Writing how the growth felt more like shrinking.

Writing how God was moving in me.

Writing how God was moving through me.

There is such beauty in releasing your control over the words God puts in your heart and just letting Him take control of the pen.

I found my truest joy in allowing Him to form analogies from the raging ocean in the Atlantic to the car ride home I had after school.

These are poems written by me for you. Every poem is something I myself have experienced. Every word is spoken through my own sufferings, my own joys, my own spiritual battles.

I pray these poems come alongside of you, give you encouragement, love, a sense of understanding.

But most of all, I pray they point you back to the One who created you, the One who breathed life into you. The One who in a crowd of five hundred people said, "Hey, you are not alone. You are worthy of the greatest of loves. My love. Step into My love."

Poems for the Lost

I began writing this section during the last semester of my senior year of high school. Up until that point in my life, I had not entirely been exposed to the dark side of high school. The partying, the drugs, the alcohol, the sex, the *everything*. I became people's go-to person for advice in these situations and, honestly, was at a loss for words. Our world is so broken; the lengths people feel desperate to run to in order to be popular, worthy, or seen broke my heart. I wrote these for the those who find themselves stuck in a pattern of constantly feeling the need to be seen by their peers.

Lost. Lost in a sea of pressure, temptation, and sin. Lost in the pull of the enemy. Lost in a cycle with feelings of no escape.

We get so enticed by the idea of temporary reward, temporary happiness, and temporary joy.

I pray these words teach you to get lost in a different type of love, to get lost in His love.

I pray you find the fulfillment that can come from being completely and utterly devoted to the King of kings.

I pray you will take a leap of faith, a dive of trust into a new life.

One of *eternal* reward, *eternal* happiness, and *eternal* joy.

*I*t can be difficult at times
To see how any of this can make sense
How a God can send His son
To live a perfect
Sinless life
To be mocked and scorned
Beaten and disowned
Judged and betrayed
And to die on a cross
To die a torturous
Painful death
For us
The beauty of it all
is that you don't have to understand
You just have to trust
Trust that in the middle of it all
He saw you
He saw you standing at his execution
In the crowd of people
He saw you and said,
"My dear beloved,
For you
I would die this death
1,000 more times."

There is a beacon of light
On a distant shore
I can feel the pull of it
The bright shimmer entices my soul
My feet make way to the curiosity
Is that you, Lord?

*T*here will always be
A thousand distractions
There will always be
An endless list of "bucket lists"
But in terms of eternity
Where do you want to be
Forever joyful
Jumping
Celebrating that He brought you
From dust to glory
On roads paved with gold
Or forever dying
Crying out to God to save you
On highways marked with fire
From earthly glory to eternal dust.

*A*nother restless day
Unending demands
Unceasing struggles
A pit in my stomach
What am I missing?
What would fill this hole?

*N*o matter the current state of your heart
No matter the thoughts that are crowding your mind
No matter the weight of the past
He is waiting for you
He is calling you
He is seeking to wrap up the mess of your mind
And transform it into His grace.

*H*e found me
Standing on the edge of the shore
He found me
In the deafening quiet of my room
He found me
in the stillness of the morning
He found me
At my lowest
He found me
With one more fight left in me
He found me
Tears streaming down my face
He found me
With an addiction
He found me
With a hopeless spirit
He found me
And He loved me
He loved me
When I couldn't say the same
He loved me
With all my baggage
He loved me
When I had nothing left to give
He loved me
And all I had to say was
"I need You."

*I*n a world
Filled with a thousand reasons to run
I pray you see the joy that can be found
In trusting in the One.

What is so beautiful to me about Christ
Is His love for me
So undeserving was I
When He picked up that cross
Looking out into the crowd of people like me
Spewing hate
Casting stones
Screaming
Crucify Him
And met eyes with me
Whispering
You
I am doing this for you.

*N*o matter the current state of your heart
No matter the thoughts that are crowding your mind
No matter the weight of the past
He is waiting for you
He is calling you
He is seeking to wrap up the mess of your mind
And transform it into His grace.

*W*hat a relief it will be
To stand at the end of the road
To look back on the different detours
To see the ways you were stretched
Stretched to the point of near breakage
But then to see the ways
He pieced you back together
What a relief it will be
To stand at the end of the road
But not to see the end of it all
To gaze past the defined way
And see the road
Goes
On.

Poems for the Strained Heart

*M*y heart goes out to the one who is fixing to read this with a heavy heart. Heartbreak is something I am quite familiar with. It is a type of pain that cannot be properly expressed into words. It is a pain so deep you feel as though you will never heal.

But God.

> He heals the brokenhearted and binds up
> their wounds. (Psalm 147:3)

I am not claiming to be an expert on how to get over the loss of a relationship, friendship, family member, spouse, mother, father, or child. I am going through this season myself. Thankfully, I do not, we do not, have to carry this burden on our own. We serve a God who is advocating on our behalf. A God who has taken all of the chipped broken pieces of our hearts and healed them. He is piecing you back together moment by moment, day by day, month by month. It is a journey.

But He is with us, and He is for us.

I pray you begin to heal from the wounds you are still trying to nurse on your own.

I pray you let the greatest Healer bind up your wounds.

I pray you give Him the ability to show you the joy that can be found in this next season of life.

A new season has begun
The hurts of yesterday
Still ever-present
The tears of today
Still falling fresh on
Your cheek
You feel helpless, lost,
Confused, hurt, afraid
But God.
His love will envelope your every need
He is good
He is here
He will never leave you
With Him, you have overcome the hardest of seasons
He was with you in the joy
And He is with you in the sorrow
Cling to Him tonight.

*T*his isn't the way you thought it would happen
This isn't the way you thought it would happen
It came out of nowhere
It was unexpected
It took your breath away
It left you in your bed for weeks
It left you in a pit you felt you could never escape
It left you questioning everything
It left you doubting your worth
It left you broken
It left you unable to pick up the pieces that lay scattered on the floor
This isn't the way you thought your life would be
This isn't the way you thought your life would be.

I pray that you see
That sometimes God must break you
In order to make you whole again
Sometimes there are seasons in your life
Where you are broken
Remember God's promise
The brokenness of one season
Can lead to the miracles in the next
God is drawing close to you tonight
He sees you
He knows you
And in Him
Your worth is immeasurable
He loves you
Every flaw
Mistake
Imperfection
He wants you
He wants you to break down the walls
You have let control your life
He wants you to lay your burdens at His feet
He wants you to rest in Him
Rest in His love.

Sit in your car
Take a moment
Mourn for the broken heart
Mourn for the destroyed relationship
Mourn for the lost friendship
Mourn for the life you thought you would have
And then
Wipe your tears
Go inside
Do not allow Satan another moment
To take you off the path
That your King has set before you.

*L*ooking back at it now
You are thankful for the season
You are thankful God revealed Himself to you
You are thankful you have grown
You are thankful the way the roads met
You are thankful for the memories that were made
You are thankful for the lessons that were learned
You are thankful above all else for Him
Looking back at it now
You smile
Hopeful of what is to come
Hopeful of what is to be.

A closed chapter
Does not mean a finished story
But a chance
To let God become the author
To let Him choose the next chapter.

I pray even today
You are seeing
That you are so much better
Wounds are mending
Your heart is being pieced back together
What once kept you locked in your room
No longer has a hold on you
Today is a new day.

*A*nd just like that
You are thankful for the road
For the lessons learned along the way
For the life that was changed
But no longer are you looking back in sadness
But looking forward in hope
For what He said He can do
And what He said He will do.

*I*t is like standing in the middle of a stormy sea
Wanting so badly to cling to the buoy right in front of you
Grasping for it in between waves
Never quite grabbing hold
Not even realizing
That there is a lighthouse in the distance
The light is calling out to you
The light is calling you home.

*O*n the days where a bowl of ice cream
Or a sad songs playlist
Isn't quite filling the emptiness in your heart
On the days where looking back at what was
Or thinking about what could have been
Isn't quite wiping the tears off your pillow
I hope you see the Father standing before you
Not rushing you
Not begging you
Just waiting
Waiting for you to see
That you are so much more than who you once were
That you are deserving of His perfect
Infinite love
I hope you see
That there is beauty
In the tear-stained pillows
There is beauty to come out of the dust.

Poems for the Healing

I think there are many misconceptions about the right way to heal. People are so quick to say, "Just get over it," or, "Wasn't that a while ago?" These words can cut deep and cause us to speed up our healing time, and we can unconsciously begin to build up walls.

In past seasons of sadness, I was constantly looking at those around me. I did not want to heal in a way that was strange or different. This mind-set caused me to take all my feelings and stuff them into a box. I had feelings of resentment toward those who I felt judged my healing. If you feel this way, you are not alone, but I have a few things I have learned that I pray make you feel more understood on your walk from broken to wholly known.

Grief does not have a timeline. Every single human has a different way of healing. Some laugh, some cry, some sleep, some scream.

Healing is different for everyone. This was a difficult pill for me to swallow. I did not understand why I could not get over the pain, why I sat with it for so long. Your journey, struggles, life are not the same as the person to your right.

Do not feel the need to compare your season of heartache to someone's season of joy. God is holding you, guiding you into greater, and it might not be what you thought it was. Trust. Trust that He is still taking you where you are meant to, just maybe on a different path.

I pray that you see that true healing can only come from Christ. There is great joy up ahead. Leave this valley and climb to the mountaintop in front of you, trusting what He says is true. Trusting that He will guide you into a new season.

*Y*ou are enough
You have so much to offer
This world
You have value
Your story is not
Finished yet
This is just one more
Valley to get through
One more page in the story
One more experience to grow from
The mountaintop is so close
You can feel the fresh air
You are a masterpiece
You are His beloved joy
When the world is telling you,
'Give up"
He is saying,
"I will give you strength"
Run to Him when it doesn't make sense
Run with Him
when tears are streaming down your face
Run to Him
when you cannot hold your head above the waters
Run to Him when all else fails
He is enough for you.

*A*s you lay your head on your pillow
Or wake up to face another day
Do not forget all the
mountains you climbed to get here
Remind yourself of the journey you are on
AL; the steps you have taken
All the ways He has carried you through
You have so much worth
So much value
Do not let this season overtake you
Smile
Pray
Breathe
Rest
You are here for a reason today
Tomorrow
The day before
The day after
Prove to the enemy that
You are a force
To be reckoned with
Because the King
Is fighting your fight.

I pray you find the strength
To move past the situations you cannot change
To be content with where you are going
And the journey He has placed you on
There are far better mountains ahead.

*I*f you find yourself struggling
To find the peace to move on
To push past
To forgive
To love in the face of hate
To give in the face of stolen time
Find it in yourself
To provide your heart with grace
The prettiest of flowers
The biggest of petals
The sweetest of buds
Often take the longest to
Bloom.

I always thought healing was a straight path
I always thought healing was a narrow road
But as seasons of suffering take root
I am beginning to see
That every day is a new day
Some days will be filled with growth and grace
Others will be plagued with pain and tears
Neither is wrong
Trusting that this is a chapter
In the book of my life
And that the Author
Has every ounce of power
To bring you where I are supposed to be.

*H*e is teaching me
That a healed heart
Does not mean a perfect heart
But a heart
That can love the next
Value the future
See the good
Trust in Him
Even when there is but one string left.

*Y*ou never understood healing
As something that would break at your heart
The same way it would restore your heart
King Jesus is in the business
Of taking all the
Tiny
Minute details
That you find yourself stuck on
And replacing them
With Him
And Him alone.

*A*round you lie
A thousand cardboard boxes
Full of different scenarios
Different lives
Different versions of you
You sift through
The memories
The joy
The pain
The laughs
The good
And the bad
You try to take all the bad
Push it all down in the smallest box
You pile up the good
Fill your hands till they overflow
Grabbing every good thing
Every smile
Every cry-turned-laugh
Every "wholly-surrendered" Jesus moment
You take off running
The good memories begin to slip
You drop one
By one
By one
Halfway down the road you look up
Meet a bright
Shining face

"Where you are going?
You will not need these anymore.
For I'm going to give you
New joyful moments
New laughs
New happiness
Leave all these here
Just let them fall
I will hold them
I will hold everything
I will hold you."

*Y*ou are stronger than you know
Even if you feel the weight of the world on your shoulders
You are braver than you feel
Even if all you can do is get out of bed
You are worthy of great love
Even if you feel used and betrayed
You are seen in a crowd of a thousand
Even if you feel like the world is passing you by
You are divinely created by the Potter
Even if you feel like a brittle piece of pottery
You are
Because He is.

The most amazing thing I have learned about healing
Is that it comes when you least expect it
You wake up one morning
And the pieces have all fallen together
The weight has been removed from your shoulders
You're able to take deeper breaths
The silly thing is though
Is that you never thought this day would come
Yet here it is in front of you
Are you going to run into this new season?
Are you going to follow Father into a fresh beginning?
You have been healed, child
Fall into grace.

Poems for the Struggling

*T*he most important thing to become aware of in your spiritual journey is the way of the road. It is easy to believe that once Christ makes home in your heart, everything will be an outpouring of sunshine and joy. That every morning you will wake up and think, "God is *good*." It is not that the phrase has lost its truth; it has just lost its volume in our lives. In times of struggle, we place God on a shelf in the far corners of our mind. We allow grief, sadness, angry, and confusion to seep into the place where He once stood. We allow flesh to overcome future. Sister, brother, friend, *listen*! God never moves farther from us. Let me repeat, King Jesus is always one step away. It is us in our human control-freak tendencies that push Him away. It is us in our weak sinful spirit who think we can handle our situations. No matter how many ways, times, or moments you try, you will never be able to handle it on your own. Give God the rule and reign in your life to surrender to Him from the very beginning. Your walk will be one of ever-winding roads, tumbling valleys, and soaring mountains. If you allow Him to, He will be there for every single joyous declaration and the millions of confused cries. I pray these poems open you up to the joys and hopes that come from your struggles. There is a purpose in your pain! There is a great reward in deep trial!

*B*efore you were born
He knew
He knew that this would be a Valley
He knew these moments would create
Aches so deep
You didn't see a way out
He knew this would cause scars on your heart
But He also knew your spirit
An unbreakable
Strong
Courageous spirit
One that no matter how many trials
No matter how many struggles
You would remain strapped in love
Bound by perfect grace
Because in the middle of it all
He knew He would hold you
Lead you
Guide you
Before you were born
He knew you
He knows you.

*T*he dark nights of deep
Deep anguish
Seem to have declared themselves
Victorious
Over the joy
Where is the Son, Lord?

*T*here is a journey
There is a road
There is a season to be discovered
There is joy
There is pain
There is heartache
There is dancing
There is music
There is silence
There is temptation
There is resistance
There is an enemy
There is a victorious King
There is a triumphant defeat
There is a comfort
There is Jesus.

The days might be dark
Before the light shines again
The nights might be long
Full of restless slumber
The months might feel like years
The struggle might be too much for you
For you
For you
But for Him
This is nothing
For Him
He can carry this weight
One-hundred times over
He wants to
He wants to take this burden
He wants you to run into freedom
He wants you to give into His love
And be alive again
He wants you to dance on the wings of surrender.

*T*his is too much
This raging sea is to vast for me
The waves continue to crash into me
The horizon is too far in the distance
You give up
Give into the tossing
Turning
Crushing blue water
You slip into the water
Slowly
But quickly
And then
A hand reaches out to you
Just above the shore
You see Him
Standing on the water
You fight
Swim till your legs give out
Reach up to the surface
Reach out to the King
He lifts you from the thunderous ocean
He places you in His arms
He rescues you
He rescues you.

*H*ealing is not a straight road
Let me say it once more
Healing is not a straight road
The road bends
The road creaks
The road has tiny cracks
Etched into its foundation
The road is long
The road seems unending
The road is daunting
I collapse into the unpaved road
I collapse into the cracks that appear
To be growing in size
I collapse into You
In You
The road is beautiful
The road has cracks
But these cracks are being filled
Filled with goodness
Filled with an immeasurable love
The longness becomes comfort
Comfort that the journey will grow me
Teach me
Transform me
I collapse into You
And You carry me onward.

I am a small flower
In the middle of a sea of bouquets
The rain comes
Those around me become drenched
Drenched in love
Renewed in spirit
Their leaves practically elevated
I receive one drop
I do not feel love
My spirit falls
My leaves are crying out
Do you see me
Do you feel my stem cracking
Do you see my roots breaking
I am in the garden
I am here
God
Do you see me.

I am trying
I am trying to keep it together
I am trying to abide in You
I am trying to shine
I am trying to stand tall
I am trying to remember the truth
I am trying
You are working
You are keeping me together
You are drawing me to You
You are shining through me
You are lifting me up
You are reminding me of the truth
You are working.

*T*he struggle is not easy
The struggle is not over
The enemy is here
The enemy is watching
The road is challenging
The road is dangerous
The goodness seems to be missing
The Father seems to be absent
The churches seem to be empty
The heart seems to be broken
The map seems to be unreadable
Where is the King of Kings
The Peacemaker is coming
The Comforter is coming
The Almighty is coming
The Savior is coming
The Sovereign One is coming
The Messiah is coming
Where is the One?
He is here.

*T*he struggle is heavy
A weight our shoulders cannot carry
The pain is sharp
A wound our body cannot heal
The tears flow constantly
A puddle our pillow cannot hold
Where is God in the darkness?
The struggle is heavy
A weight our God can carry
The pain is sharp
A wound our God can heal
The tears flow constantly
A puddle our God can hold
God is in the middle of the darkness
Brining in the light.

Poems for the Joyful

*J*oyful is my most favorite word. It is so much more powerful than "happy" or "delighted." I equate the word "joyful" with the highest of happiness. Joyfulness to me is only found in heaven. Where God kneels down and kisses our foreheads. Where the Lord sees our suffering and turns our silence into sweet symphonies. Where an orphan becomes a child of God. Where the empty becomes fulfilled. Where I become valued, worthy, seen, beautiful. Where you become His. To be joyful is to be in perfect union with the Father. I pray these poems teach you to happy dance for days on end. I pray you find true *joy* in knowing that no matter what lies ahead, no matter what has happened, and no matter where you are right now, *He loves you* with an unmatchable love.

I know there are days where it feels all hope is lost. I have had so many times where I have felt the energy just drained out of me. In these moments, we must make sure it is not our joy that has been taken away. You see, joy is *eternal.* Joy is not based on the number in your bank account. Joy is not based on the amount of followers you have on Instagram. Joy is not even based on our earthly relationships. Joy is based solely on the goodness of Christ Jesus. His death on a cross, his brutal anguishing death, served as the ultimate payment for your sin. So that the joy you experience on Earth can be eternalized in heaven. Happy dances for days on end. Happy dances for days on end thanks to His unmatchable sacrifice.

*T*here is such joy to be found
In learning that
Jesus is the only one
Who can breathe life into me
The conductor who coordinates
The symphonies of the skies
Breathes life into me.

*H*e is beginning to show you
That there is great joy
When we see the plans that He has for your life
Are far better
Than what you thought your life would be.

*A*nd so you dance
Dance to the beat of your heart
Dance to the freedom you found
Dance to the forgiveness you received
Dance to the nights you could not get up
Dance to the tears that were shed over and over again
Dance to the One who made it all possible
Dance to what could have been
Dance to what is happening now
Dance to what is to come
Dance.

*T*he joy comes
Like the sun after a rainstorm
The joy comes
Like the first flower of spring
The joy comes
Like the first time you gave into His love
The joy comes
Like the sunset after a long day
The joy comes
Like your favorite song on repeat
The joy comes
Like a good friend after a ruined relationship
The joy comes
Like a good night's sleep after a long day
The joy comes
The joy is coming.

*J*oy meets you where sorrow left you.

*G*rinning from ear to ear
Singing praises for this year
For even yesterday
You did not perceive a future
You did not perceive a hope
But here you are standing
On the wings of His good fortune
Grinning for what He has done
Grinning for what He will do.

*Y*ou called me to dance
And so I did
Pitter
Patter
On my tippy-toes
Like the child I once was
Sorrow left my heart
Doubt fled my thoughts
Anxiety coward into the corner
And joy came
Smiles pranced on my face
Happiness leapt from my fingertips
Hope filled my heart
Jesus filled my heart
You called me to dance
And so I did.

*A*nd just when I thought
The ground was too barren
Underneath my feet
Wildflowers began to bloom.

*T*he joy
The joy comes
The joy comes like rain after a dry season
The joy
The joy dances
The joy dances like a little girl playing dress up
The joy
The joy rests
The joy rests knowing it isn't going anywhere
The joy
The joy is eternal
The joy is eternal because He is eternal.

*J*oy is
Road Trips all alone
Jam sessions in my Kia
Early nights in my dorm room
Dinner in a new hole-in-the-wall
Laughter over vanilla lattes
Quiet times behind a sunset
Snuggles with family
Ice cream at all hours of the day
Cleaning out my closet
Joy is wherever I'm with You, Jesus.

Poems for the Seeking

I want to thank you for picking up this story. Whether you bought it, were given it, or found it on the side of the road, it was placed into your hands for a reason. Our great Lord works in the mightiest of ways; I can truly say I am in awe every time He makes a way in the wasteland. God is calling out to you. In the middle of your season, whether it be one of intense sorrow or newfound happiness, He desires a relationship with you. There is something so beautiful about seeking Christ. Even if it feels like you have no idea where to start, even if none of it makes sense, you are loved. Loved greater than any love you have ever experienced. Loved deeper than any love you ever will experience. Jesus Christ is in the business of giving the orphan a father, the homeless a sanctuary, the broken a healed heart, and the curious their answers. I pray that as you read this, you begin to see how great communion with Christ truly is. That no matter where you have been or where you're going, He wants you to let Him lead the way.

*M*y soul is stirring
For something deeper
My heart is aching
For someone stronger
My life is searching
For something bigger.

I see a thousand bright lights
I see an endless sea of choices
I see piles of treasures
I see mountains of joy
I see a valley full of emptiness
I see a cave of darkness
I see it all
But I don't want any of it
I just want you, Lord.

*O*ur world
Does a good job
Of leaving us empty
Like a car
One mile away from home
Running on a flashing "E" light
Our world
Does a good job
Of leaving us broken
Like a vase
Sitting on the edge of a table
Knocked off by a curious toddler
Our world
Does a good job
Of leaving us wrecked
Like a ship
Fighting to reach the shore in the middle of a storm

But our world
Is but a temporary season
A pen dot on the vast expanse
Of eternity

There is a forever on the horizon
A forever that cannot be defined by our world
That the greatest of days cannot even amount to

Forever is on the horizon.

*T*his world
This world is so broken
So evil
So empty
So I ask
Are you fulfilling?
Are you enough?
Are you everything?

The next time you start
To doubt yourself
When the words
"I am not good enough"
Start to flood your brain
Be reminded of how far
You have come
How your Savior was there
Every step of the way
How in every season
of your life you have
Overcome
The next time you start to doubt yourself
Remember your purpose
Remember His love.

S tanding on the dock
You can almost see limitless in every direction
The sky seems to fall into the waters
The stars seem to be airbrushed into the dark space
The moon sits
Almost cradled by the deep blue sky
The water lightly hits the wooden ladder under your feet
The waves gently whisper the commotion happening below
Fish of all different species slowly break the water's surface
All of this flowing in such harmony
Could this be the work of some great Creator?
Could the stars be so much more than specks of gas in the sky?
Could the same carver of roaring waves
Be the same one
Who placed a heartbeat in my chest?
Could the one who tells the ocean to dance
Be the one
Who saw fit to give me life?

*O*n the nights where
Nothing else makes sense
I pray you give into His love
Surrender to the arms of the Father
Let Him be the answer to every question.

*G*ive me a sign
In the middle of the storm
Give me a peace
In the bottom of the valley
God if You are out there
Find me in the chaos.

*T*he light in the distance
I called out to it
From behind the roaring waves
I raised my white flag
The light saw me
Reached out to me in the middle of the chaos
Rescued me from the anxiety
From the guilt
From the pride
From the idols that were keeping me chained to the floor
In a moment the light lifted me up
And loved me stronger than the waves ever could.

*A*nd it was in that moment that I began to see
What great love you had for me.

Poems for the Unsettled

*A*n unanswered prayer. A feeling of loneliness. Uncertainty. Doubt. Anxiety. I feel as though I have been here so many times. There was a period of time in my life where these feelings daily outweighed hope. I would wake up every one morning full of confidence that by the end of the day, God would intercede on behalf of my prayer. For months, I felt this hole in my heart, in my life, and in my walk with the Lord. This feeling of loneliness drove a wedge in my walk with the Lord. I felt as though He was ignoring my deepest needs, leaving me to fight the battle before me alone. I felt like a warrior going into battle without even a toothpick as a weapon.

But in those months of lonely, I found the sweetest form of dependence on the Lord. Father showed me that my strongest weapon against the enemy was the words He was speaking over me. He *is* near to the brokenhearted. He is our refuge in times of trouble. He is constant in the storm. He saw me.

When I felt unseen, He was looking into the deepest corners of my heart. He was slowly sewing back together my heart. My confidence was beginning to peak out from behind the insecurities. My tears were beginning to be masked by late night jam sessions. My joy was beginning to come from a place I never knew I needed. Before I even knew it, my prayer was answered. Before I was even able to understand where the joy was coming from, it was pouring out of me like a broken vessel. That is to the point Christ brought me to. That sometimes, the vessel must break in order to be put to use. Sometimes, the vessel must be willing to be vulnerable, show its cracks, and allow the *living water* to pour out of it.

Do not believe the lies of the enemy. If anything here is your sign, *the Father hears your prayers*! He may not answer it tomorrow, or the next day, or a year from now; continue to be faithful as He brings your needs to fruition in His timing. Fall in love with the consistent stillness of His presence.

*I*f you are lying in bed tonight
With the strings of your heart pulled
In what feels like a million directions
If you are lying in bed tonight
With the weight of doubt
Sitting heavy on your chest
If you are lying in bed tonight
With the tears of the day
Still falling fresh on your face
Breathe
Trust
Steady
His timing is not our timing
His plans will soon make sense
His voice will soon be heard.

*H*ow many more nights, Lord
How many more days will I feel
Empty
Alone
Broken
Destroyed
Nothing
Silence
And then
A knock at the door.

*H*ow foolish it was of me
To think that He would not come through
To think that He forgot me
That He abandoned me
That He no longer loved me
For in my peak season
Of distrust
In my most desperate moment
Of pure loss
He bound up my hopes and dreams
He folded them away
And He replaced them
With streams of gold.

I feel as though I should be past this by now
I feel as though every time I think
I can deeply breathe in again
I am left
Broken
Alone
It's like being in a room full of people
And feeling like you cannot be heard
No matter how many times
You yell out
No matter how many times
You wave your white flag
No one sees you
Do you see me, God?
Do you hear me?

*H*ave you not answered this prayer
Because I haven't let go
I untied my wrists from the rope
The rope that was holding me back
I thought I had dropped it
Dropped it into the deep waters
But now I see
That the rope is still being clutched
Clutched by the tips of my fingers
If I let go
Will you hear me?
Will you take away this pain?
Will you give me peace?
I want to let go of the rope
Teach me to let it go
Teach me to drop it deep into the waters
Teach me to trust
That letting go doesn't mean giving up
That letting go doesn't mean I'm forgotten
That letting go means giving into You
Giving into You
Means giving into grace.

Another day marked off the calendar
Another sleepless night
Another sip out of the bottle
Another injury to my body
Another look in the mirror
Another terrible thought
Another tear shed in the bathroom
Another half-eaten plate of food
Father
Hear my prayer
Hear my anxieties
Hear my heart
Another
Another
Another.

*D*ear God
I ask for You
To reveal yourself to me.

*T*he next time you start
To doubt yourself
When the words
"I am not good enough"
Start to flood your brain
Be reminded of how far
You have come
How your Savior was there
Every step of the way
How in every season
of your life you have
Overcome
The next time you start to doubt yourself
Remember your purpose
Remember His love.

*T*he uneasiness
Will turn back into comfort
The pain
Will turn back into joy
The confusion
Will turn into answers
Just as quickly as spring comes
After a long winter
So will the new season of life
The flower blooms despite the weather
And so will you.

*B*ut where is He in this picture?
He is in the middle of it all
He is in the between the in-between
He is in the sunshine after a rainstorm
He is in the flower bouquets after a funeral
He is in the long weekend in the middle of the semester
He is in the hug from mom after a terrible week
He is in the endless bowl of ice cream after a breakup
He is in the telephone call from the hospital
He is in the tears cried after a sleepless night
He is in the middle of it all
Hallelujah He is in the middle of it all.

Poems for the Made New

*H*ow amazing is it to be made new in Christ. How amazing is it to know that every bad day, every sleepless night, every addiction, every heartbreak, every chain *have been broken*. I am beyond words in trying to describe the great joy I feel for you, new believer!

Whether you have been said for one minute, six months, or twenty years, you are on a journey. This is one of the great, heavenly rewards. I pray even on the days you feel completely defeated that you would turn to the King. That you would allow Him to take the thoughts of the enemy captive. That you would take another step closer to the kingdom.

Remember on the days where the enemy tries to attack your newfound confidence how far you have come. You are so deserving of the Father's love, and now it is time to bring others to Him in the same way. You are a kingdom changer!

Welcome to the family, child!

*A*ll the while
I'm Beginning to see
The home and heart
You're providing me.

There will be days
When you feel
As though the whole world is against you
When you feel
The weight of pressures
The burden of doubt
The pull of desire
Know on these days most
He is standing ready
Ready to receive the win
Ready to receive the questions
Ready to receive you
You
In whatever form
Pulled together with a mask
Tears streaming down your face
Barely hanging onto the day
He wants that version of you
He wants every version of you.

*T*he pages of your story
Are beginning to be written
By the one who spoke life into existence.

As I let go of the life I thought I would have
I embrace the future fully
Knowing that all the ways
The road curved around the mountain
Has lead me to the peak
To stand tall
Looking down below
At all the places He has brought me through
And to.

$\mathcal{A}$nd now I know
Now I see
All that you have done
For me.

*T*here will be hard days
Days when the sun sits behind the clouds
There will be sleepless nights
Nights when your thoughts keep you tossing
There will be doubt
Doubt that creeps deep into your faith
But on those days
He is holding you tighter than ever before
On those days
He is the light
Barely peeking behind the clouds
On those days
He is the quiet confidence
Behind the anxious thoughts
On those days
He is the steadfast love
That is bigger than your fears.

*A*nd in that moment
I was certain
That despite the past I carried on my shoulders
He saw past it all
And wanted me.

*M*y endless doubt
Has become eternal direction
What once held me captive
Is now my victory anthem
Hallelujah to the King
For He has set me free.

*I*t all changed
It all clicked
In the midst of the unknown
I became known
No longer hiding behind the past
No longer clinging to the darkness
In the midst of the confusion
The light blinded me
The light showed me
All I could be
All He wanted me to be
In the midst of the disaster
I found my master.

*M*ay I never lose the wonder
Of what it felt to be embraced by You
For the very first time.

Poems for the Growing

I love the imagery behind flowers. The way that even by just being, they tell a story. Flowers can only stand strong when their roots are strong. If the roots of the flower aren't strong enough, the flower can be blown by the wind, uprooted, lost. We tend to be a lot like flowers. Constantly being pulled by the world, losing our footing when the going gets tough. Only when our foundation is truly built on Christ do we stand tall, unmoved by this world.

I pray that you are beginning to see the growth occurring in you is a process. That every day, you must make a choice to stand tall for Christ. Despite the wilted leaves. Despite the weary stem. For on the days where you cannot take one more gust of wind, one more pulled leaf, or one more stomped stem, that is when He is there for you the most. You are a beautiful flower, one of extraordinary capabilities. I pray you are growing wildly. That you see that Father is giving you wisdom, joy, and satisfaction in making His name known.

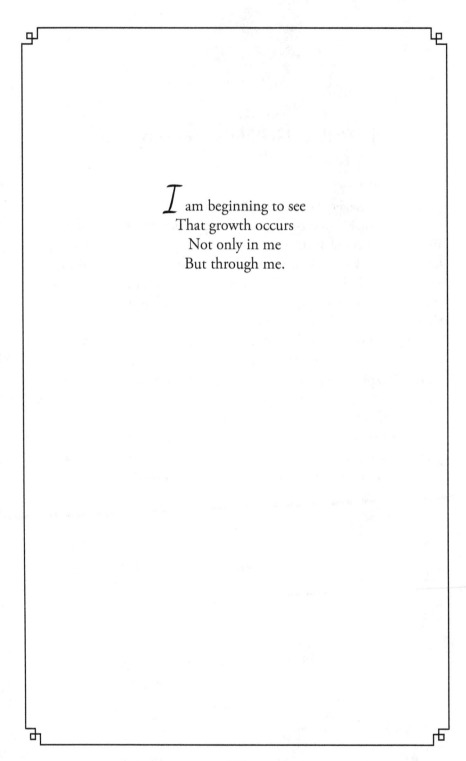

I am beginning to see
That growth occurs
Not only in me
But through me.

*T*here is beauty to be found
In seasons of growth
In looking back at the road behind
Seeing quiet moments where He was
Drawing you closer
Stretching your heart
Building your trust
For this season
There is beauty to be found
In seeing that all along
He has held you close.

*I*t is important to remember
That growth is not a temporary situation
But a lifelong journey.

*T*here are lessons
to be learned
Even in the smallest of things—
lessons from the Fig Tree.

Growth is not always about
Being the tallest you can be
Or taking up the most room in the garden
But growth is about
Taking the space He gives you
And making the flowers around you
DANCE.

A vast mountain gently covers
The field of the valley
The mountain protects from the dangers
Excessive rain
Harsh winds
The scorching sun
The mountain provides the flowers with just enough
Rain
Wind
Sun
For them to grow into who they are meant to be
Isn't that what Christ is doing for me?

*A*ll the while
Through every storm
Every drought
Every mountain you climbed
Every valley you got lost in
He was growing you
And even today
You sprouted a new leaf.

*A*nd just like that
In the blink of an eye
When your thoughts have grown silent
That He is reaching His hand down
Lifting up your wilted leaves
And calling you to bloom
Bloom bigger than you ever have before
And in that moment
You will find
You belong in this season
You belong in this life.

*F*or He is the gardener
I am the flower
Growing
Trusting
Living
Knowing that He is
Nourishing my heart
Planting seeds in my life
And watering my soul.

*A*nd you will begin to realize
That even though the music stopped
You were still dancing
The chorus fading into the back
Did not change your tempo
If anything
The rhythm began to flow out of you
Into those around you
You became the music
You struggled to hear
You became the bridge
You could never fully memorize
All because He showed you
How to use your feet.

Verses for It All

*T*his part of the book is by far the most important chapter you will read. Though I pray these words over these six chapters have been able to provide you with some level of comfort, these words in the end are meaningless. The true words that bring you ultimate satisfaction and understanding are found in God's holy word: the Bible. This little section has been added to provide you with God-breathed words for every section of poetry I have written. These are words from the Father Himself, words that I hope will cause your cup to overflow. While this book was written to truly bless your heart, I urge you to view it as a supplement and not a substitute. I thank you, reader, for the time spent with this book. For every shared feeling, emotion, and insecurity. For every exclaimed, "Me too!" For simply choosing to read it.

I will say this phrase until my lungs give out: you are worthy. Worthy of feeling deep eternal love from the Father. It has taken me many, many years to finally understand the art of being thankful for every season the Father sees fit to have me journey through. Even today as I write this, Father has revealed something to me: no matter what lies ahead, we can be joyful and content with today. As children of God, we can find confidence in the constant presence of our Father. For all the tears shed, delayed answer to prayers, and growing pains, there is a significant purpose behind the chapter being written in your life. If you are not a believer, I urge you to prayerfully consider giving your life over to Christ. It is a decision that you will never regret. Breathe these scriptures over yourself today, tomorrow, forever. The journey is long, but we are all on the road together.

You are loved, worthy, and amazing.

Jill

P.S. A special shout out to those who contributed their favorite verses to this section: thank you for playing a part in this story and inspiring those around you. You playing a piece in this story are furthering the truth that Christ has us all on this road for a purpose. We are not meant to walk this road alone. I thank you for walking this road with me and now with these readers.

Verses for the Lost

*F*or I am sure that neither death nor life, nor angels nor rulers, nor things present nor things to come, nor powers, nor height nor depth, nor anything else in all creation, will be able to separate us from the love of God in Christ Jesus our Lord. (Romans 8:38–39)

Giving thanks[a] to the Father, who has qualified you[b] to share in the inheritance of the saints in light. He has delivered us from the domain of darkness and transferred us to the kingdom of his beloved Son, in whom we have redemption, the forgiveness of sins. (Colossians 1:12–14)

I have come as a light into the world, that whoever believes in Me should not abide in darkness. (John 12:46)

I am the door. If anyone enters by Me, he will be saved, and will go in and out and find pasture. The thief does not come except to steal, and to kill, and to destroy. I have come that they may have life, and that they may have it more abundantly. (John 10:9–10)

For God so loved the world that He gave His only begotten Son, that whoever believes in

Him should not perish but have everlasting life. For God did not send His Son into the world to condemn the world, but that the world through Him might be saved. He who believes in Him is not condemned; but he who does not believe are condemned already, because he has not believed in the name of the only begotten Son of God. (John 3:16–18)

Verses for the Strained Heart

*C*ast all your anxiety on Him because He cares for you. (1 Peter 5:7)

But he said to me, "My grace is sufficient for you, for my power is made perfect in weakness." Therefore I will boast all the more gladly about my weaknesses, so that Christ's power may rest on me. (2 Corinthians 12:9)

Peace I leave with you; my peace I give you. I do not give to you as the world gives. Do not let your hearts be troubled and do not be afraid. (John 14:27)

Come to me, all you who are weary and burdened, and I will give you rest. (Matthew 11:28)

For we are his workmanship, created in Christ Jesus for good works, which God prepared beforehand that we should walk in them. (Ephesians 2:10)

Verses for the Healing

*N*o, in all these things we are more than conquerors through him who loved us. (Romans 8:37)

But they who wait for the Lord shall renew their strength; they shall mount up with wings like eagles; they shall run and not be weary; they shall walk and not faint. (Isaiah 40:31)

Rejoice in the Lord always; again I will say, rejoice. (Philippians 4:4)

For God gave us a spirit not of fear but of power and love and self-control. (2 Timothy 1:7)

Remember not the former things, nor consider the things of old. Behold, I am doing a new thing; now it springs forth, do you not perceive it? I will make a way in the wilderness and rivers in the desert. (Isaiah 43:18–19)

Verses for the Struggling

*W*hen you pass through the waters, I will be with you; and through the rivers, they shall not overwhelm you; when you walk through fire you shall not be burned, and the flame shall not consume you. (Isaiah 43:2)

For I consider that the sufferings of this present time are not worth comparing with the glory that is to be revealed to us. (Romans 8:18)

Cast your burden on the Lord, and he will sustain you; he will never permit the righteous to be moved. (Psalm 55:22)

He heals the brokenhearted and binds up their wounds. (Psalm 147:3)

I waited patiently for the Lord; he inclined to me and heard my cry. He drew me up from the pit of destruction, out of the miry bog, and set my feet upon a rock, making my steps secure. He put a new song in my mouth, a song of praise to our God. Many will see and fear, and put their trust in the Lord. (Psalm 40:1–3)

Verses for the Joyful

*T*hen he said to them, "Go your way. Eat the fat and drink sweet wine and send portions to anyone who has nothing ready, for this day is holy to our Lord. And do not be grieved, for the joy of the Lord is your strength." (Nehemiah 8:10)

The steadfast love of the Lord never ceases; his mercies never come to an end; they are new every morning; great is your faithfulness. (Lamentations 3:22–23)

Oh give thanks to the Lord, for he is good, for his steadfast love endures forever! Let the redeemed of the Lord say so, whom he has redeemed from trouble. (Psalm 107:1–2)

Surely goodness and mercy shall follow me all the days of my life, and I shall dwell in the house of the Lord forever. (Psalm 23:6)

Rejoice in the Lord always; again I will say, rejoice. Let your reasonableness be known to everyone. The Lord is at hand. (Philippians 4:4–5)

Verses for the Seeking

*F*or if you keep silent at this time, relief and deliverance will rise for the Jews from another place, but you and your father's house will perish. And who knows whether you have not come to the kingdom for such a time as this? (Esther 4:14)

Jesus said to him, "Have you believed because you have seen me? Blessed are those who have not seen and yet have believed." (John 20:29)

Then you shall call, and the Lord will answer; you shall cry, and he will say, "Here I am." (Isaiah 58:9)

"For I know the plans I have for you," declares the Lord, "plans for welfare[a] and not for evil, to give you a future and a hope. Then you will call upon me and come and pray to me, and I will hear you. You will seek me and find me, when you seek me with all your heart." (Jeremiah 29:11–13)

Let me hear in the morning of your steadfast love, for in you I trust. Make me know the way I should go, for to you I lift up my soul. (Psalm 143:8)

Verses for the Unsettled

*T*herefore I tell you, whatever you ask in prayer, believe that you have received it, and it will be yours. (Mark 11:24)

The Lord will fight for you, and you have only to be silent. (Exodus 14:14)

Trust in the Lord with all your heart, and do not lean on your own understanding. In all your ways acknowledge him, and he will make straight your paths. (Proverbs 3:5–6)

Do not be anxious about anything, but in everything by prayer and supplication with thanksgiving let your requests be made known to God. And the peace of God, which surpasses all understanding, will guard your hearts and your minds in Christ Jesus. (Philippians 4:6–7)

Rejoice in hope, be patient in tribulation, be constant in prayer. (Romans 12:12)

Verses for the Made New

*T*herefore, if anyone is in Christ, the new creation has come: The old has gone, the new is here! (2 Corinthians 5:17)

He put a new song in my mouth, a hymn of praise to our God. Many will see and fear the Lord and put their trust in him. (Psalm 40:3)

I will give them an undivided heart and put a new spirit in them; I will remove from them their heart of stone and give them a heart of flesh. (Ezekiel 11:19)

You were taught, with regard to your former way of life, to put off your old self, which is being corrupted by its deceitful desires; to be made new in the attitude of your minds; and to put on the new self, created to be like God in true righteousness and holiness. (Ephesians 4:22–24)

"The days are coming," declares the Lord, "when I will make a new covenant with the people of Israel and with the people of Judah." (Jeremiah 31:31)

Verses for the Growing

*T*hrough him then let us continually offer up a sacrifice of praise to God, that is, the fruit of lips that openly profess his name. (Hebrews 13:15)

But the fruit of the Spirit is love, joy, peace, patience, kindness, goodness, faithfulness. (Galatians 5:22)

He has told you, O man, what is good; and what does the Lord require of you but to do justice, love kindness, and to walk humbly with your God? (Micah 6:8)

Like newborn infants, long for the pure spiritual milk, that by it you may grow up into salvation. (1 Peter 2:2)

And may the Lord make you increase and abound in love for one another and for all, as we do for you. (1 Thessalonians 3:12)

About the Author

*J*illian Sigler is a work in progress very much like the book. Born in East Texas, Jillian's family soon found themselves serving in a remote community in South Sudan from the ages of thirteen to sixteen. While overseas, she began to develop a deep sense of God's calling on her life. It wasn't until her senior year of high school, however, that she became vocal about her faith and found writing as an outlet to connect with people of all walks of life.

Jillian wrapped up writing on *A Work in Progress* during her first semester of college. In university, she is studying religion with the hopes of pursuing a career that brings glory to the good news of the Gospel, in whatever capacity God calls her to.

She is passionate about the growth found in embracing the calling and plans God has for your life. Jillian hopes this book above all else is an encouragement to live life unapologetically for the Gospel. You can find more of her story and poems like these at her blog on Instagram.